Praying Exodus

The Living Word Series

Praying through the Bible, one book at a time.

Praying Exodus

Prayers for Liberation, Covenant, and the Long Journey
Home

GRAHAM JOSEPH HILL

Eagna Publishing • Sydney, Australia

PRAYING EXODUS
Prayers for Liberation, Covenant, and the Long Journey Home

Published by: Eagna Publishing (Sydney, Australia)
eagnapublishing@icloud.com
Cover and interior design: Graham Joseph Hill
www.grahamjosephhill.com

paperback isbn: 978-1-7643311-9-7
ebook isbn: 978-1-7644455-0-4
version number: 2025-12-07

NATIONAL LIBRARY OF AUSTRALIA

A catalogue record for this book is available from the National Library of Australia

Contents

Prologue: When Chains Begin to Break

Before freedom had a name,
there was only groaning in the dark.
The cries of the oppressed rose like incense,
and heaven bent low to listen.
No one saw the hidden midwives,
or the baskets floating down forgotten rivers.
But deliverance was already breathing,
Holy, loving, unseen, unstoppable.
And still the Spirit moves,
through prisons and parliaments,
through alleys, borders, and weary hearts
that ache for a different world.
The same voice that thundered from the bush
still calls through burning injustice:
"Take off your shoes. This ground is mine."
Each prayer in Exodus is a cry and a calling.
a plea for courage,
a song of uprising,
a step toward promise.
In praying Exodus,
we remember that salvation is never private,
that faith always walks beside the oppressed,
and that God still leads people out,
through the waters,
through the wilderness,
toward the wide and holy land of freedom.

1

Introduction: Praying the Deliverance

Exodus is the story of movement: from slavery to freedom, from silence to song, from despair to divine dwelling. It begins under the weight of oppression and ends with glory filling a tabernacle. Between those bookends unfolds a revelation of the God who hears cries, parts seas, feeds wanderers, and makes a home among them. Exodus is the grammar of redemption. To pray Exodus is to step into the rhythm of liberation that beats at the heart of Scripture: the holy insistence that bondage is never the final word.

Praying through Exodus awakens us to the God who delivers not only nations but hearts. We begin in Egypt, naming the chains that still bind us (fear, injustice, addiction, apathy), and we follow the long, gracious path toward freedom. Through plagues and Passover, wilderness and worship, we learn that redemption is both an event and a journey: God leading us out, God teaching us to walk, and God dwelling with us along the way.

These prayers invite encounter, not analysis. They turn history into conversation: between the enslaved and the Liberator, the wanderer and the Guide, the worshiper and the Holy One who descends in fire and cloud. As we pray Exodus, we find our own stories folded into its pages: our laments echoed in Israel's groans, our deliverance mirrored in the crossing of the sea, our worship renewed before the radiant Presence.

This book is for those longing for freedom, for courage, for renewed presence. Pray it slowly (alone or together), letting the story pray you. Let each chapter become a threshold between bondage and grace, between the God who calls us out and the God who calls us home. For Exodus isn't only Israel's story, it's ours too: a living journey from captivity to communion, from fear to freedom, from Egypt to the embrace of divine love.

The Living Word Series: A Guide to the Prayer Pattern

Each prayer in this series follows an eight-movement rhythm shaped by Scripture's own way of speaking with God.

This pattern is a pathway (flexible, honest, spacious) allowing every chapter of the Bible to breathe its truth into our lives.

I invite you to walk this rhythm slowly, letting each movement form your heart as you pray.

1. Invocation: Naming God as the Text Reveals God

Every chapter unveils a facet of God's character.

We begin by addressing God with the images, names, and actions drawn directly from the passage.

Here, prayer begins in wonder.

2. Confession: Naming Our Distortion of That Revelation

Standing before the God revealed, we acknowledge the ways we fall short: personally, communally, and systemically.

This movement is truth-telling, not shame.

3. Lament: Naming the Wounds of the World

Every text encounters a wound in creation or in us.

Here we let the chapter's sorrow speak alongside today's sufferings, refusing denial or indifference.

4. Hope in God: Turning Toward Divine Faithfulness

This is the hinge of the prayer.

We recall who God is, what God has done, and how God remains present in our lives.

Hope isn't optimism but trust.

5. Petition: Asking Boldly for Transformation

Rooted in the text's longings, we ask God to act.

We petition for justice, mercy, courage, healing: whatever the passage calls us to desire.

6. Commitment: Offering Ourselves to God's Work

> Grace invites participation.
>
> Here we pledge to walk in the light we've seen, to embody what we've prayed.

7. Eschatological Hope: Lifting Our Eyes to God's Future

> Every chapter leans toward the fullness of God's kingdom.
>
> We remember the promised renewal that holds all our prayers in hope.

8. Doxology / Assurance: Ending in Praise and Trust

> The prayer concludes in praise: naming the goodness and nearness of the Triune God.
>
> We rest in the assurance that God is faithful, now and forever.

This prayer structure mirrors the movement of the Psalms and the spiritual life itself: from naming, to truth-telling, to sorrow, to hope, to praise. The pattern holds lament and joy together so that neither becomes shallow: the honesty of pain leading us into the freedom of worship.

May this rhythm guide you as you pray your way through Scripture: honestly, courageously, and with the deep trust that the Living Word still speaks, still heals, still leads us home.

As you journey through these prayers, pause often. Let specific lines become your own. Insert the names of your community, your city, your wounds. Use silence as part of the conversation. These prayers aren't substitutes for Scripture, but doorways into it: a way to hear the ancient stories breathe again in our century.

Exodus begins in bondage and ends in glory. It assures us that the God who heard the cries of enslaved people still breaks chains, still parts seas, still makes a home among wanderers. The story moves from oppression to presence, from fear to freedom, from silence to song. May these prayers teach us to see the world as Exodus sees it: held by a God who delivers, who dwells, and who leads every captive heart toward spacious grace.

Groaning Under Pharaoh (Exodus 1)

God of the forgotten and the enslaved,
>you hear the groans beneath empire's noise,
>you see the bruises history tries to hide,
>you remember the promises buried in bondage.

We confess our comfort with oppression.
We benefit from systems that crush others,
>we turn away from injustice when it costs us nothing,
>we use technologies and goods produce on exploitation,
>we ignore human trafficking and oppression
>>when what they produce serve our desires,
>we mistake privilege for blessing and call it your will.
We're quick to pity, slow to act,
>fearful of Pharaoh or Presidents when courage is required.

We lament the cruelty that still builds our cities,
>hands that labor unseen,
>lives reduced to quotas and profit,
>children robbed of future and rest.
We mourn how fear makes tyrants,
>and apathy makes accomplices.

Yet you, O Lord, aren't silent.
You multiply life where death is decreed.
You bless the midwives who defy the throne,
>you make rebellion an act of reverence,

you begin deliverance in the often-unseen faith of women.

Even now, you raise midwives of mercy in hidden places,
> those who risk for life,
> those who speak truth in the chambers of power,
> those who cradle hope while the world forgets how to pray.

So, awaken us, God of justice.
Give us Shiphrah's courage and Puah's compassion.
Let us choose obedience to you over fear of power.
Teach us to guard life,
> to protect the vulnerable,
> to confront powers and principalities,
> to stand against systems of oppression,
> to live more simply if our abundance hurts others,
> to see your image in the oppressed.

Even now, deliver us from apathy,
> and stir our hearts to act where your people still groan.
Even now, make us restless until justice rolls and mercy reigns.

Make our compassion inconvenient,
> our faith subversive,
> our love stronger than fear.

Until every chain is broken,
> until no Pharaoh rules by terror,
> until the cries of the enslaved become songs of freedom,
> keep us faithful to your liberating mercy.

Blessed are you, Deliverer of the oppressed,
> who remembers your covenant in every generation.
Blessed are you, Christ our Exodus,

who leads captives into freedom.
Blessed are you, Spirit of courage,
who speaks "Life" in defiance of death.

Amen.

Hidden Deliverers (Exodus 2)

God of hidden beginnings,
>you watch over baskets in dangerous waters,
>you shelter fragile lives in the shadows of empire,
>you raise deliverers before the world knows their names.

We confess our impatience with your quiet work.
We want liberation without waiting,
>justice without risk,
>change without vulnerability.
We overlook the small, trembling signs of your salvation,
>the midwife's courage,
>the sister's watchful eye,
>the compassion of a foreign daughter.

We lament every child endangered by fear and violence,
>those born into poverty,
>those fleeing war,
>those hidden from systems that refuse to protect.
We mourn the families torn apart by oppression
>and the hearts that harden under the weight of cruelty.

Yet you, O Lord, are already at work
You guide the currents that carry Moses,
>you breathe courage into Miriam,
>you turn Pharaoh's palace into a sanctuary of hope.
Even now, you move behind the scenes,

weaving mercy through unexpected hands,
nurturing deliverance where the world expects despair.

So, teach us to trust your hidden ways.
Give us eyes to see your salvation in its infancy,
courage to protect the vulnerable,
and faith to believe that small acts can change the world.
Let us nurture life where fear declares death,
and partner with your quiet uprising of compassion.
Even now, stir in us the courage of Miriam,
the tenderness of Pharaoh's daughter,
and the resilience of those who refuse to bow to fear.

Make our lives places where deliverance grows,
humble, hidden, hopeful,
until your justice rises like dawn.

Until every child is safe,
until every river becomes refuge,
until freedom finds every home,
keep us faithful to your unfolding liberation.

Blessed are you, God of the hidden and the hopeful,
who begins salvation in the smallest of hands.
Blessed are you, Christ our deliverer,
who was once a child in danger.
Blessed are you, Spirit of courage,
who moves where empire can't see.

Amen.

The Name That Burns (Exodus 3)

God of unconsumed fire,
>   you blaze in ordinary bushes,
>   you call from ground we thought was barren,
>   you speak our names with a tenderness that startles us awake.

We confess our dullness to holy things.
We walk past burning wonders with hurried steps,
>   we silence the stirrings of compassion,
>   we bargain with you when you call us toward courage.
We hide behind our inadequacy,
>   believing our smallness excuses our refusal.

We lament the suffering that drew you to the bush,
>   the cries of enslaved families,
>   the weight of generational tyranny,
>   the world bent under empires that see people as quotas.
We grieve the countless places where your people still groan,
>   waiting for deliverance that seems delayed.

Yet you, O Lord, reveal yourself not in the palace but in the desert.
You bend low to listen,
>   you declare the suffering seen,
>   you kindle fire that doesn't destroy,
>   you whisper the name that holds all existence.
Even now, you ignite callings in wilderness hearts,
>   summoning reluctant prophets,

speaking liberation into the scorching silence.

So unshod our lives, O Holy One.
Strip us of our excuses,
>teach us to listen to the voice in the flame,
>and let your compassion become our courage.
Give us Moses' trembling yes,
>and the trust to follow fire wherever it leads.
Even now, speak your name through us,
>not as triumph, but as tenderness,
>not as power, but as presence.

Make us bearers of your burning mercy,
>lights in a land shadowed by oppression,
>voices that echo your cry for justice and freedom.

Until every bush burns with your glory,
>until every captive walks free,
>until your name becomes the world's healing,
>keep us faithful to the flame.

Blessed are you, I AM,
>who is present, persistent, and ablaze with love.
Blessed are you, Christ our calling,
>who turns fear into vocation.
Blessed are you, Spirit of fire,
>who burns without consuming.

Amen.

Signs in Trembling Hands (Exodus 4)

God of patient calling,
      you speak to reluctant hearts,
      you place signs in trembling hands,
      you choose the hesitant to bear the weight of your mercy.

We confess how easily fear becomes our language.
We shrink from tasks that expose our weakness,
      we plead inadequacy to escape obedience,
      we trust our limitations more than your presence.
We cling to what feels safe,
      even when you invite us into holy danger.

We lament a world still shaped by Pharaoh's terror,
      voices silenced by oppression,
      leaders who hide behind excuses,
      communities waiting for courage that never comes.
We mourn how often liberation stalls
      because we're too afraid to begin.

Yet you, O Lord, don't abandon the hesitant.
You turn staffs into serpents,
      leprous skin into living flesh,
      silence into speech,
      stammering into proclamation.
You send companions for the journey,
      and promise presence stronger than fear.

Even now, you place signs in our hands,
ordinary tools transfigured for holy work,
frail gifts kindled with your power.

So steady us, God of reassurance.
Teach us to trust what you've given,
however small, however fragile.
Let our doubts become altars of encounter,
and our weaknesses gateways for your strength.
Give us Aaron-like encouragement,
community that bears the call together.
Even now, breathe courage into our reluctance,
and let your compassion outrun our excuses.

Make us people who step forward,
not because we're confident,
but because you're faithful,
not because we feel capable,
but because the oppressed still cry out.

Until every stammer becomes a story of deliverance,
until every trembling step carries hope,
until your liberation reaches every corner of the earth,
keep us faithful to the work you place in our hands.

Blessed are you, God of signs and presence.
Blessed are you, Christ our companion on the way.
Blessed are you, Spirit of courage,
who fills trembling hearts with fire.

Amen.

When Obedience Meets Oppression (Exodus 5)

God who hears the sighs beneath our shouting,
 you send us to speak freedom
 only to find resistance tightening its grip,
  and our fears and nightmares mount,
 you call us into courage
 even when courage seems to make things worse,
  even when we struggle to trust and believe.

We confess our impatience with your timing.
We expect obedience to yield quick victories,
 justice to bloom without struggle,
 Pharaoh to tremble at your name.
When the world grows harsher instead of softer,
 we question your wisdom,
 and doubt our calling.

We lament the cruelty that follows truth-telling,
 bricks demanded without straw,
 burdens doubled on the weary,
 leaders who punish the innocent to maintain control,
 abuse and silencing that target the vulnerable,
 systems and structures that oppress and harm.
We mourn every community
 that cries, "Lord, why have you brought trouble?"
 every heart that feels betrayed by hope.

Yet you, O Lord, don't abandon the disappointed.
You listen to Moses' anguish without rebuke,
  you receive Israel's groaning as prayer,
  you hold steady when we waver.
Your promises don't shrink beneath Pharaoh's rage.
Even now, you're working in places we can't see,
  loosening chains beneath the surface,
  undermining every empire that mocks your name.

So, strengthen us, God of the long deliverance.
Keep us speaking truth
  even when our voices shake.
Teach us to trust your hidden unfolding
  when outcomes defy expectation.
Let our anger become fuel for justice,
  our confusion become deeper dependence,
  our disappointment become prayer.
Even now, plant hope in the cracks of despair,
  and remind us that every groan is heard.

Make us steadfast in the face of resistance,
  gentle when met with hostility,
  faithful when freedom feels far away.
Until oppression crumbles,
  until burdens lift from every back,
  until your word proves unbreakable,
  keep us walking toward liberation.

Blessed are you, God who hears the groaning.
Blessed are you, Christ who suffers with the oppressed.
Blessed are you, Spirit who strengthens the discouraged.
Amen.

The God Who Says "I Will" (Exodus 6)

God of outstretched arms and unbroken promise,
      you speak hope into lungs crushed by despair,
      you whisper covenant into ears deafened by suffering,
      you reveal your name not in comfort but in crisis.

We confess how quickly discouragement dims our faith.
We let harsh labors define reality,
      we trust Pharaoh's cruelty more than your compassion,
      we forget the promises spoken over our ancestors.
Weariness becomes our theology,
      and fear our preferred truth.

We lament the heaviness that makes hope hard to hear,
      spirits crushed by injustice,
      communities bowed beneath impossible demands,
      those who long for freedom yet feel abandoned by heaven.
We grieve how trauma muffles trust,
      and how suffering makes even good news sound false.

Yet you, O Lord, don't waver.
You declare your name again,
      the God who remembers,
      the God who rescues,
      the God who lifts slaves into covenant family.
You speak a future no empire can erase.
Even now, your "I will" rises above every "you can't,"

your promise pushes back against every lie of oppression,
your faithfulness stands when our strength collapses.

So, speak your name into our exhaustion.
Let your "I am the Lord" steady our trembling.
Open our hearts to hear what hope sounds like
        after years of disappointment.
Rewrite our identity as your people,
        redeemed, upheld, beloved, sent.
Even now, breathe courage into communities bowed low,
        and let your promises echo louder than their pain.

Make us midwives of your deliverance,
        bearers of covenant hope,
        servants shaped by your fierce compassion.

Until every promise finds its "yes,"
        until the oppressed stand tall,
        until your redemption fills the earth,
        keep us trusting your unfailing word.

Blessed are you, God of the "I will,"
        whose faithfulness never bends.
Blessed are you, Christ our covenant,
        who breaks chains with love.
Blessed are you, Spirit of promise,
        who sustains hope when hope seems impossible.

Amen.

Confronting the Hardened Heart (Exodus 7)

God of truth that won't flinch,
> you send your servants into the halls of power,
> you speak freedom in the face of tyranny,
> you turn staffs into signs,
> and fear into holy defiance.

We confess how easily we shrink before hardened hearts.
We prefer quiet faith to costly courage,
> respectability to resistance,
> silence to the risk of confrontation.
We tell ourselves that Pharaoh will never listen,
> so, we avoid speaking at all.

We lament the cruelty that stiffens rulers still,
> hearts calcified by wealth and empire,
> systems that defend themselves with violence,
> leaders who won't heed the cries of the oppressed.
We mourn every place where arrogance masquerades as authority,
> and every life crushed beneath its weight.

Yet you, O Lord, aren't intimidated by Pharaoh's throne.
You harden justice, not cruelty;
> you strengthen resolve, not oppression.
You raise Moses and Aaron to speak truth into a clenched world.
Your signs challenge the sorcery of empire,
> and your word stands unbroken.

Even now, you empower reluctant prophets,
        arming them not with swords,
           but with truth spoken in trembling faith.

So, embolden us, God of fearless compassion.
Teach us to confront injustice without hatred,
        to speak truth without arrogance,
        to trust your power more than our eloquence.
Let our lives become signs,
        simple, human, unmistakably yours.
Even now, soften what's hardened in us,
        and strengthen what is fearful,
        that we may stand where you send us.

Make us faithful in the face of resistance,
        gentle in the presence of anger,
        steadfast when liberation requires endurance.

Until every Pharaoh releases what he clutches,
        until every oppressed community breathes free,
        until your justice unmasks every false power,
        keep us rooted in your liberating truth.

Blessed are you, God of the outstretched arm.
Blessed are you, Christ who confronts cruelty with compassion.
Blessed are you, Spirit who emboldens prophets for the long struggle.

Amen.

When False Gods Fall Silent (Exodus 8)

God who unmasks the powers that pretend to rule,
      you expose the fragility of idols,
      you shake the foundations of empires,
      you remind the world that creation belongs to you alone.

We confess how often we bow to lesser gods.
We trust convenience more than compassion,
      productivity more than presence,
      security more than justice,
      technology more than prayer.
We cling to idols that promise control
      yet leave us restless and divided.

We lament the stubbornness that thickens hearts,
      leaders deaf to suffering,
      communities shaped by fear,
      nations trapped in cycles of exploitation.
We mourn the plagues of our own making,
      ecological wounds,
      economic injustice,
      technological captivity,
      and the social decay that follows greed.

Yet you, O Lord, make clear what Pharaoh denies.
You draw a line between deception and truth,
      between empire's sorcery and creation's God.

You reveal your power through judgments and mercy,
　　　　through signs that confront the world's false certainties.
Even now, you topple the idols we've trusted,
　　　　showing how hollow their promises are,
　　　　how fragile their grip has always been.

So, deliver us from the gods we have created.
Teach us to listen when you speak through disruption,
　　　　to discern your voice in the unraveling of false security.
Let humility soften us where pride has hardened,
　　　　and compassion awaken us where comfort has numbed.
Even now, free us from deception,
　　　　and let your truth take root in places long ruled by fear.

Make our lives testimonies to the One who liberates,
　　　　turning stubbornness into surrender,
　　　　violence into reverence,
　　　　and delusion into holy clarity.

Until every idol falls,
　　　　until every heart is open,
　　　　until your justice renews the earth,
　　　　keep us faithful to your liberating truth.

Blessed are you, God who unmasks fake power.
Blessed are you, Christ who breaks every lie with love.
Blessed are you, Spirit who clears our vision
　　　　and leads us toward freedom.

Amen.

The Weight of Unheeded Warnings (Exodus 9)

God whose voice thunders through hardened skies,
>you speak through storm and stillness,
>you warn before you wound,
>you desire repentance more than ruin.

We confess our refusal to listen.
We minimize the consequences of injustice,
>explain away the damage of our choices,
>and cling to pride even when truth confronts us.
We wait for disaster to force what humility could heal.

We lament the plagues that echo through our world,
>fields ruined by greed,
>animals suffering under human excess,
>communities crushed by policies that prize profit over people.
We mourn the stubbornness that magnifies suffering,
>the leaders who harden themselves against mercy,
>the systems that punish the innocent.

Yet you, O Lord, remain steadfast in both judgment and compassion.
You reveal your power to humble the mighty,
>your tenderness to spare the vulnerable,
>your patience in every warning you send.
Your desire isn't destruction but return.
Even now, your judgments wake us from complacency,
>your mercy calls through the cracks of calamity,

your justice shakes the foundations of pride.

So, soften our hearts before the storm arrives.
Give us wisdom to repent quickly,
        courage to change what harms,
        and humility to hear your warnings without defensiveness.
Let reverence rise where arrogance once lived,
        and obedience take root where rebellion resisted.
Even now, interrupt our stubborn patterns,
        and turn us toward your healing path.

Make us a people who bend before you,
        who seek justice before crisis,
        who choose compassion before calamity.

Until pride gives way to reverence,
        until creation rests from violence,
        until your mercy triumphs over every hardened heart,
        keep us awake to your voice.

Blessed are you, God of both mercy and might.
Blessed are you, Christ who bears judgment to bring peace.
Blessed are you, Spirit who softens stone into flesh.

Amen.

When Darkness Refuses the Light (Exodus 10)

God of dawn that no darkness can swallow,
    you confront the arrogance of kings,
    you expose the limits of every false power,
    you let the light withdraw so truth can be seen.

We confess the shadows we choose.
We cling to habits that dim our compassion,
    we prefer comfort to courage,
    we harden ourselves to truths that require change.
We pretend we can't see the suffering our choices create.

We lament the deepening darkness across our world,
    children deprived of joy,
    workers ground down by exploitation,
    communities living in the long night of injustice.
We mourn the stubbornness that refuses repentance,
    the leaders who bargain with compassion,
    the systems that keep people in generational eclipse.

Yet you, O Lord, aren't defeated by the night.
Your judgments reveal what pride tries to hide,
    your mercy persists beyond refusal,
    your liberation advances even when resisted.
You draw lines that empire can't cross,
    and light that can't be negotiated away.
Even now, your radiance presses against the darkness,

seeking cracks in hardened hearts,
calling creation back toward freedom.

So, wake us from the sleep of indifference.
Let your light rest on our consciences,
exposing what must change,
healing what fear has hidden.
Give us the courage to leave the shadows behind,
and the humility to walk where your truth guides.
Even now, illumine our choices,
and make us bearers of your relentless light.

Make us people who refuse to partner with darkness,
who advocate for the oppressed,
who stand firm when justice is at stake.

Until all the Pharaohs of the earth yield,
until light returns to every home,
until liberation dawns without obstruction,
keep us aligned with your shining mercy.

Blessed are you, Light of the world.
Blessed are you, Christ whose presence scatters night.
Blessed are you, Spirit who kindles fire in weary hearts.

Amen.

The Night Before Deliverance (Exodus 11)

God of unbearable warnings and unrelenting mercy,
  you speak truth that shakes the foundations,
  you name the cost of stubborn oppression,
  you stand in the tension between justice and grief.

We confess our fear of hard truths.
We avoid the consequences of our complicity,
  we soften what you speak in order to stay comfortable,
  we hesitate to confront systems that cause suffering.
We want freedom without disruption,
  justice without upheaval.

We lament the sorrow that judgment brings,
  the children who suffer because power refuses to bend,
  the families broken by cruelty and pride,
  the nations that cling to domination
    until grief becomes inevitable.
We mourn how the hardness of a few
  multiplies suffering for the many.

Yet you, O Lord, don't delight in destruction.
Your warnings flow from compassion,
  your judgments arise from justice,
  your desire is life and liberation.
You don't forget the cry of the oppressed,
  and you don't abandon those who wait in the dark.

Even now, you speak into the halls of Pharaoh,
    calling the powerful to yield,
    calling the enslaved to prepare for freedom.

So, teach us to hear your hard words with humility.
Give us courage to change before sorrow deepens,
    wisdom to act before harm multiplies,
    and compassion that refuses to ignore injustice's cost.
Let us stand with those awaiting deliverance,
    and resist every power that prolongs suffering.
Even now, soften what is brittle in us,
    and ready us for the freedom you're bringing.

Make us people who grieve with integrity,
    who hope with endurance,
    who act with justice,
    and who trust your heart even in heavy nights.
Until oppression releases its grip,
    until dawn breaks on every enslaved soul,
    until your liberation sweeps through the earth,
    keep us watchful for your coming.

Blessed are you, God who warns in love.
Blessed are you, Christ who bears sorrow for our freedom.
Blessed are you, Spirit who steadies us through the long night.

Amen.

The Night of Passing Over (Exodus 12)

God of sheltering mercy,
>you mark doorframes with deliverance,
>you draw a boundary death can't cross,
>you gather a captive people for a midnight exodus.

We confess how rarely we trust your strange instructions,
>the disciplines that feel costly,
>the obedience that feels inconvenient,
>the rituals that form freedom in us before we understand.

We treat your commands as burdens,
>forgetting that they're lifelines.

We lament the groaning that fills the night,
>the grief that accompanies judgment,
>the sorrow in households
>>where oppression breeds its own disaster,
>the pain that flows when power refuses to repent.

We mourn every place where violence breeds more violence,
>and where liberation comes wrapped in tears.

Yet you, O Lord, move through the darkness
>with purpose and compassion.

You protect the vulnerable with the mark of mercy,
>you redeem through a meal shared in trembling hope,
>you disrupt empires with a whisper of command.

Even now, you teach us to gather as a people,

to eat the bread of urgency,
to bind our sandals for the journey that begins at night.

So, prepare us, God of deliverance.
Teach us to trust your timing and your ways,
to receive salvation with reverent awe,
to stand ready when you call us into freedom.
Let our communities be marked by mercy,
our homes become shelters of grace,
and our tables places where liberation begins.
Even now, paint our lives with the sign of your love,
and let no darkness claim what you have redeemed.

Make us people who remember your wonders,
who walk lightly for the sake of the journey,
who refuse to return to the chains you've broken.

Until every Pharaoh releases their grip,
until every captive crosses into freedom,
until your redemption renews the whole world,
keep us faithful to your Passover mercy.

Blessed are you, God who passes over in compassion.
Blessed are you, Christ our Lamb,
whose blood shelters every seeking heart.
Blessed are you, Spirit of freedom,
who leads us out into new life.

Amen.

Led by Cloud and Fire (Exodus 13)

God who guides with light by day
       and flame by night,
       you claim your people through remembrance,
       you lead us out through unfamiliar paths,
       you walk ahead when we don't know the way.

We confess how easily we cling to what enslaves us.
We long for Egypt even as we leave it,
       we fear the wilderness more than the whip,
       we forget the cost of captivity
       and doubt the goodness of freedom.
We trust our maps more than your presence.

We lament the uncertainty that haunts new beginnings,
       the desert that feels too wide,
       the journey that feels too long,
       the memories of oppression that still echo.
We grieve the fear that keeps communities from stepping forward,
       and the voices that whisper we should return
       to what once harmed us.

Yet you, O Lord, never abandon your people.
You mark the road with pillars of mercy,
       you turn detours into deliverance,
       you lead us safely even when you lead us slowly.
Your presence is our compass,

your glory our shelter,
  your faithfulness our courage.
Even now, your light goes before us,
  illuminating steps we feared to take,
    warming hearts chilled by uncertainty.

So, guide us, God of the long journey.
Teach us to follow cloud and fire
  instead of fear and habit.
Help us remember your saving acts
  so our gratitude shapes our obedience.
Let our lives become living memorials,
  stories handed down like bread.
Even now, write your guidance on our hearts,
  and keep us attentive to your movement.

Make us people willing to travel with you,
  slowly, humbly, faithfully,
    trusting that every wilderness path
    is held in your hands.

Until every pilgrim finds rest,
  until every detour becomes redemption,
    until your presence fills every step we take,
    keep us following your light.
Blessed are you, God of fire and cloud.
Blessed are you, Christ our way through the wilderness.
Blessed are you, Spirit our ever-present guide.

Amen.

A Path Through the Impossible (Exodus 14)

God who makes a way where ways collapse,
>you hear the panic of trapped hearts,
>you stand between threat and freedom,
>you breathe wind into waters
>and carve salvation through the deep.

We confess how quickly fear unravels our trust.
We accuse you of abandonment
>when danger closes in,
>we imagine Egypt kinder than it was,
>we forget the promises carried on your breath.
We let despair speak louder than your voice.

We lament the terror that stalks the oppressed,
>armies of violence closing in,
>systems built to crush hope,
>walls of water rising on either side of fragile lives.
We grieve every community cornered by injustice,
>every soul convinced there is no escape.

Yet you, O Lord, take your stand in the narrow place.
You're the pillar behind us and the wind before us,
>the darkness that shields,
>the light that guides,
>the path that opens in defiance of death.
You turn graves into gateways.

Even now, you divide the seas that imprison us,
pushing back waters we feared would drown us,
making space for liberation to walk through on dry ground.

So, strengthen us for the steps we must take.
Teach us to stand still when fear demands frenzy,
to move when you say move,
to trust the road you open
even when it feels carved from midnight.
Let your courage enter our bones,
and your wind steady our trembling.
Even now, lead us through the impossible,
and teach us to walk in freedom's widening path.

Make us people who refuse to return to bondage,
who sing in the aftermath of deliverance,
who live as those carried through the sea by mercy.

Until every oppressor's chariot breaks,
until every trapped soul walks free,
until the world knows the God who opens oceans,
keep us walking in your wake.

Blessed are you, Waymaker and Warrior.
Blessed are you, Christ our passage through death.
Blessed are you, Spirit who breathes paths into being.

Amen.

The Song on the Far Shore (Exodus 15)

God of the shoreline where fear dissolves,
>you teach our lungs the melody of freedom,
>you turn trembling voices into choirs of triumph,
>you lift praise from the dust of danger.

We confess how rarely we stop to sing.
We rush past deliverance without gratitude,
>minimize your miracles as coincidence,
>and forget that joy is a form of obedience.
We hoard our praise when you deserve a festival.

We lament how quickly celebration fades,
>how trauma lingers after rescue,
>how new fears rise from old wounds,
>how wilderness follows even the greatest victory.
We grieve the battles still raging in the hearts of the freed,
>and the enemies that lurk behind memory's shadows.

Yet you, O Lord, delight in the songs of the rescued.
You shatter the chariots that seemed invincible,
>you drown the arrogance of empire in your justice,
>you lead your people to stand on solid ground
>with still hearts and astonished joy.
You invite us to remember in rhythm and refrain.
Even now, you teach us harmonies of hope,
>melodies that carry courage into tomorrow,

songs that refuse to forget what you have done.

So, tune our hearts to gratitude.
Let Miriam's tambourine echo in our steps,
    let Moses' song rise in our breath,
    let praise become the pulse of our faith.
Help us sing on days when joy feels costly,
    and on days when praise comes naturally as breathing.
Even now, place new songs on our tongues,
    songs strong enough to steady us for the wilderness ahead.

Make us a people who remember through singing,
    who resist despair with melody,
    who proclaim your triumph with tenderness and truth.

Until every sea gives way to freedom,
    until every oppressor falls silent,
    until your whole creation joins the song,
    keep us singing on the far shore.

Blessed are you, God of the victorious song.
Blessed are you, Christ our salvation's refrain.
Blessed are you, Spirit who teaches us to praise.

Amen.

Bread for the Restless (Exodus 16)

God who feeds wanderers in wide deserts,
      you hear our hunger before we speak it,
      you answer grumbling with grace,
      you rain bread on ground that once felt barren.

We confess the restlessness that rules our appetites.
We demand certainty while refusing trust,
      we complain more easily than we give thanks,
      we long for the comforts of Egypt
      even when they chained us.
We store up what you meant to be shared,
      hoarding out of fear rather than hope.

We lament the ache of unmet needs,
      families unsure where the next meal will come from,
      communities hollowed by scarcity,
      workers worn down by systems that never let them rest.
We grieve the hunger, physical and spiritual,
      that stalks your people still,
      and the impatience that rises when wilderness stretches too long.

Yet you, O Lord, provide with tenderness and precision.
You send manna that spoils if hoarded,
      quail that arrives in the quiet of evening,
      rest woven into the rhythm of the days.
You teach us daily trust,

daily dependence,

daily wonder.

Even now, you scatter grace like dew,

feeding us in ways we didn't know to ask for,

satisfying us with mercies shaped for this very day.

So, train our hearts for your provision.

Teach us to gather without greed,

to rest without guilt,

to trust you when our cupboards feel thin.

Let our gratitude outgrow our anxiety,

and our sharing outpace our fear.

Even now, loosen our grip on what we cling to,

and open our hands to the generosity of your kingdom.

Make us a people sustained by your daily bread,

content in your timing,

patient in your leading,

joyful in your care.

Until hunger is no more,

until every wilderness becomes a banquet,

until your Sabbath peace settles over all creation,

keep us near the One who feeds his people.

Blessed are you, God of manna and mercy.

Blessed are you, Christ our living bread.

Blessed are you, Spirit who nourishes and renews.

Amen.

Water From the Rock (Exodus 17)

God who meets us at the edge of our endurance,
> you hear the crack in our voices before the complaint forms,
> you see the dryness in our spirits,
> you stand beside us
>> when thirst makes us doubt everything we knew of you.

We confess how quickly scarcity distorts our trust.
We accuse you of abandonment when you're near,
> we test your patience instead of remembering your kindness,
> we turn on one another when fear runs high.
We forget every time you've brought us through before.

We lament the thirst that haunts your people still,
> communities without clean water,
> families parched for justice,
> souls wandering through seasons that offer no relief.
We grieve the conflicts that rise when pressure mounts,
> and the anger that erupts when hope feels thin.

Yet you, O Lord, don't abandon the thirsty.
You stand on the rock before us,
> you command life to burst from unyielding stone,
> you turn barren places into fountains of mercy.
Your provision isn't delayed,
> it arrives at the exact moment despair believes it's too late.
Even now, you strike the rock of our fear,

letting generosity flow through what we thought was empty,
bringing water to the weary and dignity to the desperate.

So, satisfy us again, God of living waters.
Quench the dryness of our hearts,
heal the fractures in our communities,
teach us to trust your provision more than our panic.
Let your peace interrupt our arguments,
and your presence steady our trembling.
Even now, soften what is brittle in us,
and make streams flow in the deserts we carry.

Make us people who drink deeply of your grace,
peacemakers when conflict rises,
hope-bearers in parched places,
servants who trust the One who stands on the rock.

Until thirst is no more,
until justice flows like a river,
until peace becomes the banner over every nation,
keep us near your life-giving mercy.

Blessed are you, God our rock and water.
Blessed are you, Christ our living stream.
Blessed are you, Spirit who refreshes every weary heart.

Amen.

Wisdom in the Wilderness (Exodus 18)

God who sends counsel at the perfect hour,
      you meet us in the strain of our calling,
      you bring companions to steady our trembling hands,
      you shape communities through voices we did not expect.

We confess the pride that isolates us.
We cling to tasks we should release,
      we pretend to carry burdens alone,
      we mistrust the wisdom offered by others,
      and confuse exhaustion with faithfulness.
We forget that your work was never meant to rest
          on one set of shoulders.

We lament the fractures that come from overwork,
      leaders burnt thin,
      teams stretched past breaking,
      communities weary because their shepherds are weary.
We grieve the harm that grows when counsel is ignored,
      and the loneliness that haunts those
          who try to do everything themselves.

Yet you, O Lord, weave wisdom into our path.
You speak through fathers-in-law and friends,
      through seasoned mentors and quiet observers,
      through those who love us enough to tell the truth.
You teach us that shared leadership isn't weakness but mercy,

that discernment is a gift,
and that sustainability is a form of obedience.
Even now, you send Jethro voices into our wilderness,
voices that steadied before,
voices that still can lead us toward health.

So, humble us, God of communal strength.
Open our ears to counsel shaped by compassion,
open our hands to share the burdens we carry,
open our hearts to trust the gifts you've given others.
Teach us rhythms of delegation,
patterns of rest,
habits of mutual care.
Even now, guide us toward wisdom that protects,
and leadership that breathes life instead of draining it.

Make us a people who lead together,
patiently, prayerfully, generously,
honoring each gift in the body,
building communities that flourish in shared grace.

Until every burden is rightly held,
until your people thrive in healthy service,
until wisdom becomes our common language,
keep us receptive to the guidance you send.

Blessed are you, God of counsel.
Blessed are you, Christ our wise shepherd.
Blessed are you, Spirit who teaches us the way of shared strength.

Amen.

Called to the Mountain (Exodus 19)

God of thundered promise and tender approach,
　　　　you summon us to holy heights,
　　　　you wrap mountains in cloud and fire,
　　　　you speak a covenant that reshapes identity,
　　　　you call wanderers a priestly people.

We confess how easily awe fades from our hearts.
We grow casual with the sacred,
　　　　treating your presence like a familiar habit,
　　　　forgetting the weight of glory that once made the earth tremble.
We try to domesticate you,
　　　　to keep you close enough to comfort
　　　　but far enough not to confront.

We lament how distant we often feel,
　　　　not because you withdraw,
　　　　but because fear or shame keeps us at the foot of the mountain.
We grieve how doubt clouds our vision,
　　　　how cynicism dulls our reverence,
　　　　how the noise of our world makes it hard to hear your voice.

Yet you, O Lord, descend in holiness without destroying.
You draw near with fire that purifies, not consumes;
　　　　you cradle your commands in love;
　　　　you speak identity before expectation.

You call us treasured,
  set apart,
  a people who bear your heart in the world.
Even now, your voice gathers us,
  inviting us up the mountain,
  inviting us into covenant,
  inviting us to become what your love declares.

So ready us for your presence.
Still our fears,
  steady our trembling,
  clear our minds to hear what you speak.
Give us reverence without terror,
  obedience without legalism,
  joy that rises from being chosen.
Even now, shape us into a priestly people,
  bridging heaven and earth with compassion.

Make us bearers of your holiness,
  not as superiority,
  but as service;
  not as distance,
  but as welcome;
  not as pride,
  but as love ablaze with mercy.

Until all peoples hear your voice,
  until every nation knows your nearness,
  until the whole earth becomes your dwelling place,
  keep us faithful at the foot of your mountain.

Blessed are you, God who descends in glory.
Blessed are you, Christ who fulfills the covenant.

Blessed are you, Spirit who writes the law upon our hearts.

Amen.

The Words That Set Us Free (Exodus 20)

God who speaks from fire and cloud,
> you give commandments not to crush us
> but to teach us how to live,
> how to breathe as a liberated people,
> how to become what freedom requires.

We confess how easily we misuse freedom.
We return to the idols we once renounced,
> we shape you in our image,
> we treat your name lightly,
> we refuse the rest you command,
> we harm our neighbors with thoughtless words
> and wounded loyalties.
We make small the law meant to make us whole.

We lament the harm caused when your ways are ignored,
> families fractured by violence or neglect,
> communities poisoned by deceit,
> lives diminished by theft or exploitation,
> relationships scarred by unfaithfulness,
> a world weakened by greed and disregard.
We grieve the wounds that follow when we choose autonomy over love.

Yet you, O Lord, speak law as an act of tenderness.
You free us from the tyranny of our desires,
> you anchor our restless hearts,

you teach us the contours of belonging.
Your commands are windows into your character,
        invitations into a life shaped by mercy and justice.
Even now, your voice thunders gently,
        calling us back to the path that leads to flourishing,
        calling us to a holiness that heals.

So, inscribe your Word upon our lives.
Form our desires in your wisdom,
        our habits in your compassion,
        our relationships in your truth.
Teach us to honor what you honor
        and cherish what you cherish.
Even now, reorder our lives around your goodness,
        and let obedience become our joy.

Make us a people who embody the Ten Words,
        worshiping with undivided hearts,
        resting as resistance,
        loving neighbors as kin,
        protecting the vulnerable with fierce tenderness.

Until your law is written on every heart,
        until justice and mercy kiss,
        until your kingdom comes in fullness,
        keep us faithful to your liberating Word.

Blessed are you, God who speaks life.
Blessed are you, Christ who fulfills every command with love.
Blessed are you, Spirit who writes the law upon our hearts.

Amen.

Justice With a Human Face (Exodus 21)

God who intertwines justice into the ordinary,
> you care for servants and strangers,
> for the wounded and the wronged,
> for those whose lives unfold far from courts and kings.

We confess how easily we overlook the small places
> where justice matters most.
We speak loudly about righteousness
> while ignoring the daily indignities our neighbors bear.
We minimize harm when it's convenient,
> excuse violence when it benefits us,
> and forget that reverence for you is measured
> by how we treat the vulnerable.

We lament the wounds that echo through households and streets,
> violence disguised as power,
> abuse tolerated in hidden corners,
> lives diminished by systems that forget compassion.
We grieve communities where justice is uneven,
> where the poor have little recourse,
> and where dignity is often the first thing stolen.

Yet you, O Lord, dignify every life.
You write compassion into law,
> protect the injured with fierce clarity,
> constrain vengeance with mercy,

47

and insist that every person,

      slave, stranger, widow, worker,

      bears your image.

Your justice isn't abstract but embodied.

Even now, you call us to a righteousness

      that touches real people, real wounds, real lives.

So, form us in your humane justice.

Teach us to protect the vulnerable with vigilance,

      to restrain our anger,

      to repair harm rather than amplify it,

      to seek restoration where others seek retribution.

Let compassion be our instinct,

      and fairness our daily practice.

Even now, correct our blind spots,

      and make us courageous in the face of everyday injustice.

Make us a people who honor dignity in every encounter,

      who listen before we judge,

      who defend those without voice,

      who act with wisdom, mercy, and humility.

Until justice rolls like a river,

      until every life is guarded with tenderness,

      until your kingdom's compassion shapes our common life,

      keep us faithful to your ways.

Blessed are you, God of the vulnerable.

Blessed are you, Christ who heals what violence has broken.

Blessed are you, Spirit who teaches us the justice of love.

Amen.

Compassion in the Details (Exodus 22)

God who sees every hidden wrong and every act of kindness,
>you reveal justice through the small, ordinary exchanges of life,
>you defend the stranger and the stranger's child,
>you shelter widows and those left without defenders,
>you shape a community where mercy is the measure of holiness.

We confess how easily we separate faith from the everyday.
We minimize harm when it benefits us,
>we treat restitution as optional,
>we overlook the pain our actions cause,
>and forget that the poor are your particular treasure.
We justify ourselves when compassion feels inconvenient.

We lament the wounds that ripple through communities,
>debts that crush the vulnerable,
>exploitation hiding behind contracts,
>property valued more than people,
>kindness lost in the scramble for advantage.
We mourn every life diminished by injustice practiced in the shadows.

Yet you, O Lord, bind compassion to justice.
You command restitution that restores dignity,
>protection for those without power,
>restraint for those with it.
You forbid exploitation and sanctify empathy.
You insist that holiness be visible in how we treat the least among us.

Even now, you speak through these ancient laws,
    calling us into a justice that protects,
    into a mercy that repairs,
    into a love that knows no stranger.

So, school our hearts in your compassion.
Teach us to make wrongs right,
    to care for those easily forgotten,
    to refuse vengeance,
    to act with fairness shaped by tenderness.
Let generosity replace grasping,
    and humility undo arrogance.
Even now, attune us to the cries of the vulnerable,
    and ready us to answer with courage and love.

Make us a people whose everyday lives embody your justice,
    whose words heal rather than harm,
    whose debts build dignity,
    whose mercy reveals your heart.

Until exploitation is no more,
    until compassion shapes every law and every home,
    until your kingdom's justice nourishes the earth,
    keep us faithful to your ways.

Blessed are you, God of the vulnerable.
Blessed are you, Christ who restores what has been taken.
Blessed are you, Spirit who forms mercy deep within us.

Amen.

Justice That Welcomes and Rest That Heals
(Exodus 23)

God who writes mercy into the very structure of life,
>you command justice that reaches beyond convenience,
>rest that interrupts exploitation,
>and hospitality that mirrors your own generous heart.

We confess the shortcuts we take with justice.
We lean toward the powerful instead of the vulnerable,
>favor familiar voices over truthful ones,
>twist fairness when it serves our interests,
>and neglect the rest we need in order to love well.

We forget that holiness is revealed in how we treat the least.

We lament the injustices that still scar our world,
>the poor denied protection,
>the foreigner met with suspicion or disdain,
>workers strained by relentless demands,
>land exhausted by greed,
>communities fractured by partiality and vengeance.

Yet you, O Lord, insist on a different way.
You command truth even when it costs us,
>mercy that disrupts cycles of harm,

Sabbath that heals creation and workers alike,
>and hospitality that dismantles fear.

You promise to go before us,
>an angel guarding our steps,

a presence stronger than our enemies.
Even now, you lead us into a justice both tender and courageous,
a mercy large enough to embrace the stranger,
a rest wide enough to heal the weary.

So, reshape our instincts, God of truth and tenderness.
Teach us to resist bribery and favoritism,
to defend those without advocates,
to love the outsider as kin,
to honor the Sabbath as your gift and our liberation.
Let our justice be fair,
our mercy generous,
our rest restorative.
Even now, guide us by your presence,
and keep us from paths that harm.

Make us a people whose lives reveal your character,
slow to harm, quick to help,
steady in truth,
restful in trust,
bold in welcome.

Until justice flows freely,
until the weary rejoice in rest,
until the stranger is embraced without fear,
keep us close to the One who goes before us.

Blessed are you, God of truth and rest.
Blessed are you, Christ our guide and guardian.
Blessed are you, Spirit who teaches us the justice of love.

Amen.

Into the Cloud of Glory (Exodus 24)

God whose presence shimmers on mountain heights,
>> you call your people into covenant,
>> you seal promises with blood and blessing,
>> you let elders see your radiance
>> and invite us to dine at your table.

We confess our reluctance to enter deeper places with you.
We prefer clarity to cloud,
>> safety to nearness,
>> ritual to relationship.
We say "All that the Lord has spoken, we will do,"
>> yet our obedience wavers when the mountain grows steep.
We forget the cost and beauty of covenant life.

We lament the distance we often choose,
>> the fear that keeps us from intimacy,
>> the distractions that keep us from worship,
>> the doubts that prevent us from ascending.
We grieve how rarely we linger in your presence,
>> content with glimpses when you offer glory.

Yet you, O Lord, come close in fire and cloud.
You reveal yourself not only to prophets,
>> but to ordinary elders with trembling hands.
You dwell among your people,
>> invite us into communion,

and call us into the mystery where revelation blooms.
Even now, your voice calls us higher,
> into the cloud that conceals and reveals,
> into the covenant that binds us with love,
> into the presence that transforms.

So, draw us near, God of holy ascent.
Teach us reverence without fear,
> obedience without rigidity,
> wonder that steadies rather than overwhelms.
Let your Word shape our commitments,
> your presence renew our courage,
> your glory kindle our worship.
Even now, lead us into the cloud
> where your nearness becomes our nourishment.

Make us a people who keep covenant,
> trustworthy in our promises,
> faithful in our worship,
> joyful in your presence,
> bold in following wherever you lead.

Until the whole earth becomes your dwelling,
> until every table becomes a place of communion,
> until every heart beholds your glory,
> keep us climbing toward you.

Blessed are you, God of covenant and cloud.
Blessed are you, Christ who brings us to the mountain.
Blessed are you, Spirit who reveals the glory of God.

Amen.

A Dwelling Made of Willing Hearts (Exodus 25)

God who chooses to dwell not in palaces but among pilgrims,
     you ask for offerings shaped by joy,
     you gather gold and acacia and fabric dyed with wonder,
     you design a sanctuary where holiness can be held
        in human hands.

We confess how often we build for ourselves instead of for you.
We seek grandeur more than presence,
     efficiency more than reverence,
     success more than beauty.
We hoard what you meant to be shared,
     and offer you only what costs us nothing.

We lament the spaces where your dwelling is obscured,
     communities fractured by pride,
     sanctuaries stripped of compassion,
     leaders who forget that holiness lives among the humble.
We grieve when the church becomes a monument
     rather than a meeting place for your mercy.

Yet you, O Lord, still desire to pitch your tent among us.
You call for offerings that rise from willing hearts,
     you weave beauty into worship,
     you fashion sacred spaces
        from human hands and divine imagination.
Your presence isn't contained but welcomed,

not demanded but invited.
Even now, you ask us to build with generosity,
      to craft spaces where love dwells,
      to prepare room for glory to rest.

So gather our gifts, God of the abiding presence.
Take our gold and our grief,
      our linen and our longing,
      our skill and our surrender.
Shape our generosity into a home for your holiness.
Even now, stir in us a willingness that reflects your heart,
      and make our offerings a place where you delight to dwell.

Make us a people who build sanctuaries,
      not only with materials,
      but with compassion;
      not only with craftsmanship,
      but with justice;
      not only with beauty,
      but with welcome.

Until every place becomes a dwelling for your glory,
      until every heart becomes an ark of your presence,
      until the whole earth becomes your tabernacle,
      keep us building with you.

Blessed are you, God who chooses to dwell.
Blessed are you, Christ our living sanctuary
Blessed are you, Spirit who fills our offering with glory.

Amen.

Beauty That Holds Your Presence (Exodus 26)

God whose dwelling is stitched with wonder,
> you wrap holiness in curtains of blue and purple and crimson,
> you frame mystery with acacia and gold,
> you teach us that sacred space
>> is crafted with patience and reverence.

We confess how carelessly we treat what is holy.
We rush where we should linger,
> we improvise where you ask for intention,
> we grow bored with beauty meant to awaken us.
We prefer efficiency to craftsmanship,
> and convenience to careful love.

We lament the places where reverence has thinned,
> sanctuaries stripped of beauty,
> communities that hurry past your presence,
> spirits dulled by distraction and haste.
We mourn how easily we lose sight of glory
> when we forget the practice of attending to you.

Yet you, O Lord, teach us another way.
You dwell within the layered tent,
> hidden yet near,
> mysterious yet intimate.
You reveal that the sacred isn't found in luxury
> but in faithful detail,

not in spectacle but in devotion.
Even now, you invite us to craft lives
        stitched with beauty and intention,
        rooms where your presence can rest.

So shape us, God of the sanctuary within.
Give us patience to build slowly,
        reverence to build beautifully,
        and love to build hospitably.
Let every curtain of our lives
        be dyed with compassion,
        every frame strengthened with integrity,
        every space prepared with longing for you.
Even now, teach us to host your holiness
        with the tenderness it deserves.

Make us a people who create dwelling places for your glory,
        homes marked by peace,
        communities shaped by care,
        hearts attuned to your presence, even in hidden rooms.

Until every life becomes a living tabernacle,
        until the world is layered with beauty again,
        until your presence fills all things,
        keep us crafting what welcomes you.

Blessed are you, God of the sacred tent.
Blessed are you, Christ our veil and our access.
Blessed are you, Spirit who fills every sacred space.

Amen.

An Altar in the Open Court (Exodus 27)

God who meets us in the wide places,
>> you set an altar at the heart of our gathering,
>> you invite us into a courtyard open to heaven,
>> you teach us that holiness isn't hidden but hospitable.

We confess how easily we distort worship.
We offer you what costs us nothing,
>> we guard what you ask us to release,
>> we forget that sacrifice is meant to shape our love.
We approach your presence casually,
>> forgetting the fire that purifies and restores.

We lament the ways worship has been twisted,
>> made performative instead of sincere,
>> transactional instead of transformative,
>> exclusive instead of welcoming.
We mourn sanctuaries where some feel uninvited,
>> and altars where justice and mercy are forgotten.

Yet you, O Lord, build a courtyard large enough for all who seek you.
You fashion an altar strong enough to carry our failures,
>> your fire consumes what harms us,
>> your grace receives what we surrender.
You gather us not to shame but to renew,
>> not to intimidate but to welcome.
Even now, you open space for us,

a place where burdens can be released,
where wounds can be tended,
where hearts can be restored by your flame.

So draw us to your altar with honesty.
Teach us to bring our true selves,
our griefs and our gratitude,
our sins and our longings.
Let our sacrifices be shaped by love,
our offerings be rooted in justice,
our worship be filled with humility and joy.
Even now, kindle in us a fire
that burns away pretense
and illuminates compassion.

Make us a people whose worship invites others near,
whose courtyards are open,
whose altars are places of reconciliation,
whose gatherings echo your welcome.

Until every barrier falls,
until every heart finds home in your presence,
until your fire refines the whole earth,
keep us faithful in your courtyard of grace.

Blessed are you, God of altar and mercy.
Blessed are you, Christ our sacrifice of love.
Blessed are you, Spirit who keeps the flame alive.

Amen.

Clothed for Holy Work (Exodus 28)

God who clothes your servants with beauty and burden,
      you weave holiness into fabric and thread,
      you set precious stones upon the shoulders of the willing,
      you engrave every name upon the breastpiece of love.

We confess how lightly we treat the calling to serve.
We rush into ministry without reverence,
      or shrink back from it with fear.
We forget that leadership is intercession,
      that honor is responsibility,
      that your people are to be carried with tenderness.
We seek attention instead of obedience,
      glory instead of compassion.

We lament the ways spiritual leadership has been distorted,
      garments once meant for beauty turned to symbols of power,
      positions meant for service twisted into control,
      communities wounded by those who forgot whom they carry.
We grieve the names dropped,
      the stories ignored,
      the hearts forgotten by those entrusted to love them.

Yet you, O Lord, restore dignity to the calling.
You dress your servants not in superiority
      but in remembrance.
You place the names of the people over the heart,

you set them upon the shoulders for bearing,
　　　　you crown service with holiness and humility.
Even now, you clothe us for the work you entrust,
　　　　threading compassion into our vocation,
　　　　placing your people close to our hearts,
　　　　adorning our weakness with grace.

So robe us in your beauty, God of holy garments.
Dress us in patience and truth,
　　　　fasten humility upon our shoulders,
　　　　let compassion be the fabric of our ministry.
Teach us to carry one another faithfully,
　　　　to remember every name entrusted to our care,
　　　　to serve not as performers but as intercessors.
Even now, fit us for holy work
　　　　with the dignity that comes only from you.

Make us a people who wear your presence well,
　　　　whose lives shine with mercy,
　　　　whose leadership reflects your tenderness,
　　　　whose service reveals your heart.

Until every servant is clothed with joy,
　　　　until every community is carried with love,
　　　　until your glory rests upon all your people,
　　　　keep us robed in your grace.

Blessed are you, God who clothes the called.
Blessed are you, Christ our great high priest.
Blessed are you, Spirit who adorns us with holiness.

Amen.

Consecrated for Your Presence (Exodus 29)

God who sets hearts and hands apart for holy work,
>	you call ordinary people into extraordinary nearness,
>	you consecrate through water and oil,
>	through offering and blessing,
>	through rituals that form us in ways our hurried minds resist.

We confess our impatience with the slow work of holiness.
We want transformation without surrender,
>	anointing without sacrifice,
>	authority without humility.
We rush past the practices that shape our character,
>	and treat consecration as ceremony rather than calling.

We lament the wounds caused when unformed leaders lead,
>	communities harmed by pride or carelessness,
>	ministries built on charisma rather than compassion,
>	altars tended by hands too hurried to love well.
We grieve the harm done when we serve without being grounded,
>	and the pain multiplied by leaders who forget your ways.

Yet you, O Lord, consecrate with care.
You cleanse and clothe your servants,
>	you anoint them with oil that carries fragrance and meaning,
>	you sanctify them through daily offerings,
>	morning and evening,
>	faithful and unglamorous, steady as breath.

Your holiness isn't a flash but a formation.
Even now, you call us into rhythms that make us whole,
      practices that anchor our wandering hearts,
      and sacrifices that reorder our desires.

So consecrate us again, God of gentle remaking.
Wash what has grown dull,
      anoint what has grown weary,
      set apart what has been distracted or divided.
Teach us to serve with clean hands and quiet courage,
      to carry your presence with reverence,
      to offer ourselves daily,
      as willingly as the morning lamb,
      as faithfully as the evening one.
Even now, shape us through repeated surrender
      until our lives bear the fragrance of your love.

Make us a people set apart for mercy,
      steadfast in compassion,
      humble in service,
      joyful in obedience,
      faithful in the slow, sacred work you entrust to us.

Until holiness becomes our home,
      until your presence dwells among us fully,
      until your glory fills all that we offer,
      keep consecrating us in love.

Blessed are you, God who forms your servants.
Blessed are you, Christ our consecration and sacrifice.
Blessed are you, Spirit who anoints and sustains.

Amen.

The Fragrance of Nearness (Exodus 30)

God whose presence rises like fragrance through the sanctuary,
    you command incense to fill the holy place,
    you cleanse hands and hearts with water,
    you remember your people through atonement
    that turns guilt into grace and distance into nearness.

We confess how faint our prayers often are.
We let distraction snuff out devotion,
    we forget the beauty of meeting you,
    we approach your presence casually,
    and grow numb to the cost of reconciliation.
We settle for stale routines
    when you invite us into living communion.

We lament the places where prayer has grown cold,
    altars unattended,
    leaders weary of intercession,
    communities tired of waiting,
    souls longing for the scent of mercy again.
We mourn the estrangement that sin creates,
    and the ways unhealed wounds linger in the spirit.

Yet you, O Lord, draw us back through beauty and grace.
You call for incense to rise morning and evening,
    a steady reminder that prayer is breath and belonging.
You provide cleansing for the work we must do,

atonement for the burdens we can't bear.
Your presence fills the sacred spaces we prepare.
Even now, you invite us to breathe again,
    to lift our lives like fragrance,
    to let mercy perfume the rooms we inhabit.

So draw us near, God of smoke and sweetness.
Cleanse our hands for service,
    cleanse our hearts for love,
    cleanse our imaginations for wonder.
Let our prayers rise without hurry,
    without pretense,
    without fear.
Even now, kindle in us a persistent intercession,
    steady as incense,
    gentle as grace,
    bold as your compassion.

Make us a people whose lives smell like mercy,
    whose prayers create sanctuary,
    whose worship softens hardened hearts,
    whose presence carries the aroma of Christ.

Until every breath is prayer,
    until every heart is washed clean,
    until the world is filled with the fragrance of your nearness,
    keep us faithful in the holy place.

Blessed are you, God of cleansing and communion.
Blessed are you, Christ our atonement and fragrance.
Blessed are you, Spirit who fills the air with your peace.

Amen.

Crafted by the Spirit (Exodus 31)

God who breathes wisdom into human hands,
>you fill artisans with imagination,
>you inspire builders and weavers with divine skill,
>you shape beauty through willing hearts,
>and crown your commands with the gift of rest.

We confess our narrow view of what is holy.
We separate craft from calling,
>art from worship,
>labor from love.
We strive without Sabbath,
>work without wonder,
>and forget that creativity is a language you speak.

We lament the ways our work has been twisted,
>creativity commodified,
>craft exploited,
>workers drained without mercy,
>rest dismissed as weakness.
We mourn beauty neglected,
>gifts unused,
>communities robbed of the artistry that makes life humane.

Yet you, O Lord, choose artisans for your dwelling.
You anoint Bezaleel and Oholiab with your Spirit,
>imbuing skill with holy purpose,

marrying craftsmanship with devotion.
You command Sabbath,

> the rest that refuses Pharaoh's pace,
>
> the pause that protects our humanity.

Even now, you fill your people with gifts

> meant to bless, to build, to beautify,
>
> meant to reflect the creativity of your heart.

So anoint our work, God of artistry and rest.
Consecrate our hands for compassion,

> our minds for wisdom,
>
> our crafts for glory.

Teach us to labor without striving,

> to create without ego,
>
> to rest without guilt.

Let our work echo your imagination,

> and our rest embody your peace.

Even now, stir dormant gifts to life,

> and make our communities sanctuaries of creativity and
Sabbath.

Make us a people who build with love,

> steadily, beautifully, collaboratively;
>
> who create spaces where your presence can dwell;
>
> who honor rest as deeply as we honor work.

Until your kingdom shines with the artistry of justice,

> until every gift serves mercy,
>
> until all creation becomes a sanctuary of rest and beauty,
>
> keep shaping us by your Spirit.

Blessed are you, God who inspires.
Blessed are you, Christ whose work redeems.

Blessed are you, Spirit who creates and renews.

Amen.

When We Shape Our Own Gods (Exodus 32)

God whose glory can't be fashioned by human hands,
    you call us to wait in trust,
    to listen for your voice from the heights,
    to live from the covenant you have written in love.

We confess how quickly we grow impatient with your silence.
We forge idols from our fears,
    shape golden calves from our longings,
    seek visible certainty instead of invisible faith.
We worship what reflects us
    rather than what transforms us.
We bow to our own making
    when you call us to your mystery.

We lament the ruin idolatry brings,
    communities fractured by false worship,
    leaders pressured into compromise,
    joy warped into chaos,
    trust shattered by betrayal.
We mourn how easily we trade your presence
    for something glittering and hollow.

Yet you, O Lord, don't abandon us to our folly.
You listen to the intercession of your servants,
    you temper judgment with mercy,
    you remember your promises even when we forget ours.

You call Moses down the mountain with both grief and grace,
        ready to restore what we have broken.
Even now, your mercy rises faster than our rebellion,
      your patience outlasts our wandering,
      your compassion reaches into our self-made ruins.

So break our idols, God of unmaking and renewal.
Shatter whatever steals our trust,
      expose whatever demands our devotion,
      free us from the gods that devour us.
Give us hearts that wait instead of wander,
      ears that listen instead of panic,
      faith that outlasts every silence.
Even now, rebuild us with your mercy,
      and restore us through your steadfast love.

Make us a people who rise from repentance,
      humble in leadership,
      faithful in worship,
      undaunted in intercession,
      steadfast in covenant love.

Until idolatry is undone,
      until trust is our truest offering,
      until your presence is our only worship,
      keep us anchored in your mercy.

Blessed are you, God who forgives.
Blessed are you, Christ who intercedes for us.
Blessed are you, Spirit who turns our hearts back to you.

Amen.

If Your Presence Doesn't Go With Us (Exodus 33)

God whose nearness is our only true courage,
      you speak to your servant face to face,
      you pitch your presence outside the camp
      and invite seekers to come and sit in the quiet glow.
You remind us that the journey is nothing
      without you walking beside us.

We confess how often we settle for your gifts instead of your presence.
We chase success without intimacy,
      mission without prayer,
      progress without communion.
We rely on strategies rather than Spirit,
      on reputation rather than relationship.
We want the promised land
      more than we want the God who promised it.

We lament the loneliness of leadership,
      the weight that blinds us,
      the fear that we might go on without you.
We grieve communities content with distance,
      content with second-hand faith,
      content with angels when you offer yourself.

Yet you, O Lord, draw near to those who seek your face.
You honor Moses' bold plea,

you reveal mercy as your glory,
         you promise your presence as the true inheritance.
You carve out a cleft of safety
         so that your radiance doesn't destroy, but restores.
Even now, you whisper, "My presence will go with you,"
         offering rest deeper than progress,
         companionship stronger than fear.

So teach us to yearn for you above all else.
Make prayer our tent of meeting,
         desire our altar,
         obedience our path.
Let our boldness ask only for more of you,
         your ways, your heart, your nearness.
Even now, hide us in the cleft of your kindness,
         and let your goodness pass before us.

Make us a people shaped by presence,
         slow to hurry,
         quick to listen,
         radiant with the afterglow of encounter.

Until your glory fills every wilderness path,
         until your nearness becomes the world's healing,
         until we're home in your presence forever,
         keep us walking with you.

Blessed are you, God who goes with us.
Blessed are you, Christ who reveals the Father's glory.
Blessed are you, Spirit who dwells within and among us.

Amen.

The Name That Renews Us (Exodus 34)

God whose name glimmers with mercy,
>   you descend in cloud and proclaim yourself in tenderness,
>   you pass before your servant with compassion,
>   you bind your glory not to power but to steadfast love.

We confess how poorly we have carried your name.
We speak of you without resembling you,
>   proclaim grace while withholding it,
>   brandish truth without kindness,
>   rush to anger though you're slow to it.
We forget that those who bear your name
>   must bear your character too.

We lament the wounds caused when your name is misrepresented,
>   religion wielded as weapon,
>   communities shaped by fear instead of mercy,
>   leaders who claim your authority but not your heart.
We grieve every place where your glory is obscured
>   by our lack of compassion.

Yet you, O Lord, reveal yourself again and again.
Merciful and gracious,
>   slow to anger,
>   overflowing with steadfast love and faithfulness.
You renew the covenant we have fractured,
>   you rewrite the tablets we have broken,

you allow your radiance to linger on human faces.
Even now, your goodness passes before us,
    calling us into a love that heals
        what judgment alone could never restore.

So carve your name into our lives.
Let mercy shape our speech,
    patience guide our decisions,
    faithfulness steady our commitments.
Make our presence a reflection of yours,
    our character a window into your heart.
Even now, shine your radiance into our shadows,
    that we may bear the glow
        of those who have stood in your presence.

Make us a people of renewed covenant,
    quick to forgive,
    slow to harm,
    eager to show compassion,
    zealous for justice shaped by love.

Until your steadfast love renews all creation,
    until every heart knows your name,
    until the world is radiant with your glory,
    keep revealing yourself to us.

Blessed are you, God of mercy and truth.
Blessed are you, Christ whose face shines with the Father's compassion.
Blessed are you, Spirit who transforms us from glory to glory.

Amen.

Hearts Stirred to Build (Exodus 35)

God who awakens generosity in weary people,
>you stir hearts with holy desire,
>you loosen hands long clenched by fear,
>you gather artisans, elders, and laborers
>into a single act of worship and building.

We confess the reluctance that grips us.
We hold tightly what you ask us to release,
>we protect our resources more than your mission,
>we underestimate the beauty our gifts could create,
>and we forget that offering is joy, not loss.

We lament the communities where generosity has cooled,
>visions stalled by scarcity,
>creativity quenched by apathy,
>gifts unshared because trust has eroded.
We grieve every place where fear has replaced freedom,
>and where the work of your kingdom suffers
>because hearts have grown guarded.

Yet you, O Lord, call forth abundance from unexpected places.
You bless the willing,
>inspire the skilled,
>and knit together a community carrying treasure in their hands.
You don't impose generosity, you awaken it.
And when your people respond,

your dwelling rises from obedient hearts.
Even now, you stir your church to build,
      not monuments but mercy,
      not temples of pride but places of presence.

So move among us, God of the willing heart.
Loosen what we cling to,
      kindle imagination in our artisans,
      enlarge generosity in our leaders,
      and anchor trust in your provision.
Let giving become delight,
      and craftsmanship become prayer.
Even now, breathe a shared purpose into your people,
      that we may build what shelters your glory.

Make us a community shaped by joyful offering,
      eager to share,
      glad to participate,
      bold to imagine,
      faithful to create with you.

Until your dwelling fills every neighborhood,
      until generosity becomes our native language,
      until your people build with beauty and love,
      keep stirring our hearts to give.

Blessed are you, God who inspires the willing.
Blessed are you, Christ who offers all for us.
Blessed are you, Spirit who fills our hands with skill and grace.

Amen.

When Generosity Overflows (Exodus 36)

God who turns willing hearts into abundance,
      you inspire gifts beyond measure,
      you call artisans to build with devotion,
      you teach your people that enough is a holy word,
      and that your dwelling rises from shared love.

We confess our fear that there won't be enough.
We hoard what you mean to multiply,
      we doubt your provision,
      we cling to scarcity even when generosity surrounds us.
We mistrust the craftsmanship you've placed within us,
      believing our gifts too small for your glory.

We lament communities shaped more by fear than generosity,
      visions abandoned for lack of trust,
      ministries starved by hesitancy,
      work left unfinished because hearts were never stirred.
We grieve every time suspicion silences generosity
      and every place where "not enough" becomes a story
      we tell more often than your faithfulness.

Yet you, O Lord, delight in overflow.
You move your people to give freely,
      to bring so much that Moses must say,
         "Stop, there is more than enough."
You empower artisans to build with accuracy and beauty,

you transform offerings into sanctuary,
you turn human willingness into divine presence.
Even now, you awaken abundance in unexpected places,
inviting us to trust the God who multiplies and sustains.

So teach us the freedom of enough.
Make generosity our instinct,
craftsmanship our joy,
cooperation our witness,
and trust our daily rhythm.
Let the work of our hands be steady,
our giving be cheerful,
our hearts be aligned with your dwelling desire.
Even now, loosen our grip on what we store,
and strengthen our grip on what we build together with you.

Make us a people who overflow in mercy,
whose generosity surprises,
whose craftsmanship blesses,
whose unity creates sanctuaries of peace.

Until there is more than enough for every need,
until scarcity becomes a broken lie,
until your presence fills the work of our hands,
keep us building with joy.

Blessed are you, God of abundance.
Blessed are you, Christ our sufficiency.
Blessed are you, Spirit who makes our offerings overflow.

Amen.

Vessels for Your Nearness (Exodus 37)

God whose presence rests among crafted things,
    you inspire hands to shape gold into mercy,
    wood into witness,
    lamps into light,
    and altar into rising prayer.
You let human artisans build what will hold your holiness.

We confess how lightly we treat what hosts your presence.
We hurry past the work of forming beauty,
    we treat worship as convenience,
    we forget that craftsmanship is devotion
    and that reverence is revealed in details.
We overlook the sacredness of the ordinary skill
    you place in human hands.

We lament the ways beauty has been neglected,
    sanctuaries stripped of wonder,
    communities built without care,
    work done without love,
    lives shaped without attention to what's holy.
We grieve how easily the lamp of our hearts grows dim
    when we no longer tend it with faithfulness.

Yet you, O Lord, fill ordinary workers with extraordinary purpose.
You guide Bezaleel's hands as he crafts the ark of testimony,
    you spark imagination for lampstands of almond blossom,

you shape a table meant for fellowship,
you fashion an altar for incense
that carries prayer into your presence.
Even now, you entrust us with the work
of shaping spaces where you may dwell,
of tending lights that refuse to go out,
of forming beauty that reflects your glory.

So awaken our craftsmanship, God of holy detail.
Let us build with love, shape with patience, serve with precision,
and honor your presence in every task.
May our work become prayer,
our creativity become offering,
our spaces become sanctuaries.
Even now, teach us to hold your glory
with humility, care, and joy.

Make us vessels for your nearness,
lives that carry mercy,
hearts that shine with holy light,
communities fragrant with prayer
and steady with faithfulness.

Until all creation becomes your dwelling place,
until every craft reveals your beauty,
until your presence fills what our hands have shaped,
keep forming us in wonder.

Blessed are you, God of beauty.
Blessed are you, Christ who dwells among us.
Blessed are you, Spirit who inspires every holy work.

Amen.

Holiness in the Open Court (Exodus 38)

God who meets us in unroofed spaces,
>you let your glory dwell not only in the sanctuary
>but in the open court where everyday feet gather,
>where the altar burns steady,
>and where basins brim with cleansing for the weary.

We confess how often we privatize your presence.
We wall off holiness as if it belongs to a few,
>we forget that worship spills into courtyards and streets,
>we treat sacred work as the task of specialists
>rather than the calling of a willing people.
We overlook the everyday offerings that sustain your dwelling.

We lament the places where open spaces have become barriers,
>communities guarded instead of welcoming,
>altars approached with fear rather than trust,
>acts of service burdened by pride or fatigue.
We grieve how many feel uninvited into the holy,
>as though your courtyard were too narrow for their story.

Yet you, O Lord, widen the space where you meet your people.
You gather bronze from the mirrors of women who served,
>you shape basins for cleansing,
>you anchor altars with sacrifice that opens paths to life.
You craft holiness not in seclusion but in community.
Even now, you call us into the open court,

to stand in your light,

to be washed by mercy,

to offer what we carry with willing hands.

So draw us into your spacious presence.

Cleanse what has grown dusty,

purify what has grown jaded,

receive what we place upon your altar.

Let our offerings be honest,

our service be joyful,

our welcome be wide.

Even now, enlarge our hearts

that your holiness might shine through our hospitality.

Make us a people who build open courtyards,

where the weary find cleansing,

where the fearful find courage,

where the overlooked find honor,

and where every offering becomes part of your dwelling.

Until your sanctuary stretches across the earth,

until every life is washed in mercy,

until your presence fills all open places,

keep us faithful in the work of welcome.

Blessed are you, God of the open court.

Blessed are you, Christ our cleansing and our altar.

Blessed are you, Spirit who widens our hearts.

Amen.

Garments for Glory (Exodus 39)

God who crowns obedience with beauty,
      you invite ordinary hands to stitch holiness into fabric,
      you weave gold into thread and dignity into calling,
      you clothe your servants so they may carry your presence
      with reverence and joy.

We confess how easily we treat obedience as burden rather than gift.
We rush past the details that shape devotion,
      we grow careless with the work that reveals your glory,
      we prefer shortcuts to craftsmanship,
      and we forget that every stitch of faithfulness matters.

We lament the ways beauty is neglected in your name,
      worship stripped of wonder,
      service drained of joy,
      ministry done without tenderness or care.
We grieve leaders who forget the weight of their garments,
      and communities that fail to honor their calling.

Yet you, O Lord, delight in the work of willing hearts.
You bless the artisans who follow your pattern exactly,
      you rejoice in garments made with devotion,
      you allow beauty to become a sign of your presence.
You clothe your people not for spectacle
      but for service, compassion, and intercession.
Even now, you're adorning your church,

threading glory into ordinary faithfulness,
dressing us for the work you entrust,
granting dignity to every act of obedience.

So clothe us anew, God of holy garments.
Cover our impatience with your patience,
our carelessness with your wisdom,
our self-reliance with your humility.
Let us wear compassion like linen,
justice like a sash,
mercy like a radiant crown.
Even now, tailor our lives to fit your calling,
and adorn us with the beauty of holiness.

Make us a people who honor the work of your hands,
crafting beauty that reflects your heart,
serving with dignity,
worshiping with wonder,
living as those dressed for your presence.

Until all creation is robed in glory,
until every life shines with your radiance,
until your dwelling is complete among your people,
keep perfecting the work begun in us.

Blessed are you, God who clothes with splendor.
Blessed are you, Christ our garment of righteousness.
Blessed are you, Spirit who adorns the church in holiness.

Amen.

When Glory Fills the Tent (Exodus 40)

God who finishes what you begin,
>
> you raise the dwelling through willing hands,
>
> you breathe glory into crafted spaces,
>
> you take your place among a people still learning to trust.

Your radiance becomes their compass,

> your nearness their shelter in the wilderness.

We confess how quickly we forget that you desire to dwell with us.

We treat your presence as occasional,

> your leading as optional,
>
> your glory as something we must earn.

We try to live by our own light

> even as your cloud stands ready to guide.

We lament the places where your presence feels obscured,

> communities wandering without direction,
>
> hearts yearning for guidance but unsure how to wait,
>
> leaders tired of uncertainty,
>
> pilgrims who can't see the next step.

We grieve the wilderness seasons

> when your glory feels distant or hidden.

Yet you, O Lord, remain faithful.

You fill the tent with a radiance no one can manufacture,

> you surround your people with cloud and fire,
>
> you lead not from afar but from the very center of their life.

Your presence moves when it's time to journey
  and rests when it's time to stay.
Even now, you pitch your tent among us,
    dwelling in our midst,
    guiding us with quiet clarity,
    holding us together with your light.

So dwell with us, God of the traveling sanctuary.
Fill our lives with a glory that steadies our fear,
    a presence that anchors our wandering,
    a guidance that doesn't rush or delay.
Teach us to move when you rise,
    and to rest when you remain.
Even now, let your nearness become our courage
    and your glory our path.

Make us a people who travel by your light,
    attentive, trusting, humble,
    living as those accompanied by holiness.

Until your glory fills all creation,
    until every wilderness becomes home,
    until you dwell with humanity forever,
    keep us beneath your cloud and within your fire.

Blessed are you, God who dwells.
Blessed are you, Christ our tabernacle.
Blessed are you, Spirit who fills us with glory.

Amen.

The Glory Dwelling Among Us: A Prayer for the Whole of Exodus

God of fire and cloud,
>you've led us through deep waters and wandering wastes,
>through deserts of fear and mountains of meeting.

You've fed us with mystery,
>given law to shape our love,
>and pitched your tent among our restless hearts.

We give you thanks for every deliverance,
>the ones we noticed,
>and the ones we did not.

You've broken our chains,
>taught us to walk upright,
>and turned our murmuring into songs of trust.

Even now, you lead your people onward.
Even now, you kindle pillars of courage
>to guide us through the night.

You dwell not only in tabernacles of gold,
>but in every act of mercy,
>every heart that shelters another in your name.

We confess that freedom frightens us.
We prefer the comfort of Egypt to the risk of promise.
But you, O Lord, keep moving,
>teaching us that faith is a journey,

and worship is a way of life.

So, send us forth, O God of Exodus,
    with manna of mercy and water of grace.
Make our communities signs of your presence,
        our homes small sanctuaries of peace,
        our work a continuation of your redemption.

Until every desert blooms,
        until all creation becomes your dwelling place,
        until the whole earth shines with your glory,
        keep us following the pillar of your presence.

Blessed are you, God who leads and stays,
        whose glory fills the wilderness.
Blessed are you, Christ our deliverer,
        whose mercy makes a way through the sea.
Blessed are you, Spirit of promise,
        whose fire still burns among your people.

Amen.

Benediction: To Those Who Keep Walking Free

Go now, children of freedom and fire.
Walk in the path once marked by cloud and flame.
Carry the memory of waters parted
        and the taste of manna that still sustains the weary.
Let your steps echo the song of the liberated,
        the song that begins in groaning
        and ends in gratitude.
Remember the God who delivers and dwells,
        who leads not only to promise,
        but through wilderness.
The One who writes law upon the heart,
        who fills tents of dust with glory,
        who turns complaint into communion.
Let your life become a pillar of mercy,
        your words a shelter for the fearful,
        your faith a flame that guides others home.
And when the road stretches on through silence,
        remember: the Presence still goes before you,
        and the Glory still rests behind.
The journey isn't over; the covenant isn't broken.
The fire hasn't gone out.
Even now, the wilderness blooms,
        and God walks among the freed.
Go in peace and keep walking with God.
Amen.

Appendix 1: Would You Help?

Writing a book takes immense effort. It's a sustained labor of love over months, even years. Every page carries hours of thought, prayer, revision, and hope. And while the writing may be solitary, the life of a book is communal. That's where you come in. If this book has meant something to you, I'd be deeply grateful if you could help it find its way into more hands and hearts.

There are two simple but powerful ways you can do that.

First, consider leaving a short review on Amazon (and Goodreads would be wonderful too). Even just a few sentences can help others discover the book, as reviews significantly influence how books are recommended and shared online. You can do that by visiting Amazon or searching for this book and writing a review. Even a short note helps people find the book.

Second, if the book has stirred something in you, would you share it with others: friends, groups, churches, or anyone who might benefit from its message?

Your support helps keep this work going, and it means more than I can say. Thank you for being part of this journey.

Find this book on these pages:

1. Amazon:

https://www.amazon.com.au/stores/author/B008NI4ORQ

2. Goodreads:

https://www.goodreads.com/author/show/20347171.Graham_Joseph _Hill

3. Author Website:
https://grahamjosephhill.com/books/

Appendix 2: About Me

Graham Joseph Hill (OAM, PhD) is an Adjunct Research Fellow and Associate Professor at Charles Sturt University, and one of Australia's most prolific and awarded Christian authors. He's written more than twenty books, including *Salt, Light, and a City*, which was named Jesus Creed's 2012 Book of the Year (church category); *Healing Our Broken Humanity* (with Grace Ji-Sun Kim), named Outreach Magazine's 2019 Resource of the Year (culture category); and *World Christianity*, shortlisted for the 2025 Australian Christian Book of the Year. In 2024, Graham was awarded the Medal of the Order of Australia (OAM) for his service to theological education. He lives in Sydney with his wife, Shyn.

Author and Ministry Websites

GrahamJosephHill.com

GrahamJosephHill.Substack.com

youtube.com/@GrahamJosephHill_Author

Linktr.ee/dailydevotions

facebook.com/grahamjosephhill/

instagram.com/grahamjosephhill/

amazon.com.au/stores/author/B008NI4ORQ

goodreads.com/author/show/20347171.Graham_Joseph_Hill

Books

See all my books at GrahamJosephHill.com/books

Appendix 3: Connect With Me

I'd love to stay connected with you. You can sign up to my Substack, Spirituality and Society with Hilly, where I share new writing, spiritual reflections, and updates on future books. Please find me on Substack: https://grahamjosephhill.substack.com

You can also find my books on my website: https://grahamjosephhill.com/books

You can also connect with me through my Facebook author page: https://www.facebook.com/GrahamJosephHill/

www.ingramcontent.com/pod-product-compliance
Lightning Source LLC
Chambersburg PA
CBHW031326040426
42443CB00005B/230